89781

D1263293

November

by Mari Kesselring
Illustrated by Ronnie Rooney

Content Consultant:
Susan Kesselring, MA
Literacy Educator and Preschool Director

magic wagon

visit us at www.abdopublishing.com

Published by Magic Wagon, a division of the ABDO Group, 8000 West 78th Street, Edina, Minnesota 55439. Copyright © 2010 by Abdo Consulting Group, Inc. International copyrights reserved in all countries. All rights reserved. No part of this book may be reproduced in any form without written permission from the publisher.

Looking Glass Library™ is a trademark and logo of Magic Wagon.

Printed in the United States.

Text by Mari Kesselring
Illustrations by Ronnie Rooney
Edited by Holly Saari
Interior layout and design by Emily Love
Cover design by Emily Love

Library of Congress Cataloging-in-Publication Data

Kesselring, Mari.
  November / by Mari Kesselring ; illustrated by Ronnie Rooney ; content consultant, Susan Kesselring.
     p. cm. — (Months of the year)
  ISBN 978-1-60270-638-5
 1. November—Juvenile literature. 2. Calendar—Juvenile literature. I. Rooney, Ronnie, ill. II. Kesselring, Susan. III. Title.
  CE13.K48 2010
  398'.33—dc22
                              2008050703

Do you know the 12 months of the year?

It's a good time to learn. Let's get in gear!

The eleventh month
is a great month to learn.
Do you know its name?
Take a guess. It's your turn!

Long ago November was
month number 9.
Now it's month 11,
and that is just fine.

6

November has 30 days—
lots of time to rake leaves.
This fall chore cleans up
under the trees.

Election Day in November
is like a big contest.
Grown-ups vote for a leader
they think is the best.

November 11
is Veterans Day.
We thank the armed forces.
Hear what they say.

A big feast for Thanksgiving
helps us remember
Pilgrim and Indian friends
who shared a meal in November.

November is about more than turkey and pie.

It is raisin bread month.

Give it a try!

National Novel Writing Month
is a November event.
Ask your classmates what kinds
of stories they invent!

Gather your friends
for a game of football.
It's an outdoor sport
that people play in the fall.

Whew!

It is finally the end of November.

Do you know what month is next?

It is December!

Vote!

Election Day is in November. See if you can set up a voting booth in your classroom. Vote for someone you want to be in charge of something.

Draw a Turkey

A big part of Thanksgiving is turkey. Get out some markers or crayons and a piece of paper. Trace your hand for the feathers and head of the turkey. Color it in and hang it up as a Thanksgiving decoration!

Words to Know

armed forces—the army, navy, air force, and marines.
December—the twelfth month of the year. It comes after November.
election—when people vote to decide who will be in charge.
gust—a big wind.
veteran—a person who has served in the army, navy, air force, or marines.

Web Sites

To learn more about November, visit ABDO Group online at **www.abdopublishing.com**. Web sites about November are featured on our Book Links page. These links are routinely monitored and updated to provide the most current information available.